Victoria

Flower Style

Arrangements for Every Occasion

Diane Wagner

HEARST BOOKS
A division of Sterling Publishing Co., Inc.

New York / London
www.sterlingpublishing.com

Illustrations by Diane Wagner

Photo Credits:

Front Cover: Robert Gattullo
Back Cover (left to right): Toshi Otsuki (2); Jim Bastardo; Toshi Otsuki

Jim Bastardo – 98 (all)
Richard Brown – 11 (top),15, 77 (top)
Pierre Chanteau – 47 (all), 49
Pieter Estersohn – 126
Robert Gattullo – 4, 9 (top; bottom), 10 (2nd from top), 18, 20 - 22, 24, 27-35, 54, 60 - 61, 80, 86 - 87,107 - 108,114 - 115, 139
John Glover – 10 (2nd from bottom),12 (top),129
Toshi Otsuki – 1, 9 (2nd from bottom), 13 (2nd from bottom), 16, 44, 50 (all), 56 (bottom), 66, 69 (all), 71, 74, 77 (bottom), 79, 85, 89, 92, 94, 95, 103, 111, 113, 117, 122, 130, 133, 134, 135, 137, 140
Luciana Pampalone - 6
Steven Randazzo - 41
Laura Resen - 101
Michael Skott – 37, 39, 51, 52, 56 (top), 59, 63
William Steele – 10 (bottom),102 (all),120, 125,136
iStockphoto – 8 (all), 9 (2nd from top),10 (top),11 (2nd from top; bottom) 12 (2nd from top; bottom), 13 (top; 2nd from top; bottom), 14 (all)

Library of Congress Cataloging-in-Publication Data
Wagner, Diane, 1951-
  Victoria : flower style : arrangements for every occasion / Diane Wagner.
      p. cm.
  Includes bibliographical references and index.
  ISBN-13: 978-1-58816-631-9 (alk. paper) ISBN-10: 1-58816-631-7 (alk. paper)
  I. Victoria magazine (San Clemente, Calif.) II. Title. III. Title: Flower style.
  SB449.W24 2008

    745.92—dc22

                              2007032431

    10 9 8 7 6 5 4 3 2 1

Book design by Anna Christian

Published by Hearst Books, A Division of Sterling Publishing Co., Inc.
387 Park Avenue South, New York, NY 10016

Victoria and Hearst Books are trademarks of Hearst Communications, Inc.

For information about custom editions, special sales, premium and corporate purchases, please contact Sterling Special Sales Department at 800-805-5489 or specialsales@sterlingpub.com.

Distributed in Canada by Sterling Publishing
c/o Canadian Manda Group, 165 Dufferin Street, Toronto, Ontario, Canada M6K 3H6

Distributed in Australia by Capricorn Link (Australia) Pty. Ltd.
P.O. Box 704, Windsor, NSW 2756 Australia

Manufactured in China

Sterling ISBN 13: 978-1-58816-631-9
       ISBN 10: 1-58816-631-7

Contents

Dedication

To R.G. for unfailing support

To E.G. for constant inspiration

D.W.

Introduction

As a long-time admirer of *Victoria* (and an occasional contributor to its editorial pages), I was thrilled to be given the opportunity to create this book. Searching through the archives of beautiful photographs, I became reacquainted with some of my favorite features. I have presented these floral designs in an easy-to-use format so you can create the same arrangements in your own home.

The step-by-step instructions take the mystery out of designing with flowers. The floral arrangements themselves were chosen to provide challenges at all skill levels. If you are a beginner, start with something simple like the colorful summer bouquet on page 66 or the charming nosegay on page 125 and leave the wedding flowers to the more experienced.

Each project is identified with a floral design skill level: basic, moderate, or advanced. Basic projects will get you started with simply arranged bouquets in containers filled with water or floral foam. Moderate design skills needed for the next level of projects involve more sophisticated combinations of floral materials while more complex construction techniques such as chicken wire over floral foam are reserved for use in advanced projects. Bridal bouquets and other projects that require close attention to detailed floral placement fall into the advanced category as well.

I hope you will be encouraged to expand your creative efforts by experimenting with different flowers and other natural materials. The floral list for each project can be customized to your individual color preferences and budget or changed to suit seasonal availability.

This project has been a pleasure at every step and I thank my editor, Maryanne Bannon, for her enthusiasm from start to finish. Most of all—I hope you enjoy using the book as much as I have enjoyed writing it.

Diane Wagner

dianewagnerdesigns.com

all about flowers

Flowers should be a daily presence in everyone's life. A simple bouquet in the kitchen or on the coffee table adds cheeriness, color, fragrance, and seasonal detail to your home. An arrangement made for a holiday or a special occasion gives a very personal touch to the celebration and sets the tone for your table and decorations. Having flowers around just makes everyone feel good.

When choosing cut flowers from a florist or grower, select blooms with buds that are beginning to open and show signs of color. Properly conditioned, the flowers will open so you can enjoy them for the longest possible time. If you purchase flowers that are already fully open, the petals may soon start to drop. If you purchase buds that are too tightly closed, they may never open. You should see the edges of rose petals and tulips should be ready to burst with color. One exception is lilies. The green buds almost always open. As each flower opens and then withers, the next bud on the stem will flower. Good-quality Casablanca lilies can give you up to two weeks of fragrant blooms.

You should always take the time to properly condition your floral purchases to get the longest possible life from each stem of flowers. Clean water and a freshly cut stem are the most important elements of floral conditioning.

HARDY FLOWERS

The wide variety of hardy flowers that are available year-round offers an abundant selection for every occasion. Most of these flowers have strong stems that take up water well, making them suitable for long-lasting arrangements. They are good choices for use in wet floral foam. Asters, snapdragons, yarrow, and dill won't wilt on an outdoor summer table. An urn of hardy mums placed in an entry foyer will hold up to cool autumn breezes from an open door. A favorite bowl filled with roses and a few tendrils of ivy makes a coffee-table centerpiece that will last all week. The following is a list of hardy focal flowers that provide strong, colorful interest in arrangements.

ALSTROEMERIA

ALSTROEMERIA These open well to create a large colorful head of small lilylike flowers.

ASTER Many colors including very pretty shades of pink and purple, extremely long lasting.

CARNATION Large single-stemmed and miniature varieties come in an array of colors, including variegated tones and lacy-edged petals.

CHRYSANTHEMUM

CHRYSANTHEMUM The mum family offers a huge selection of colors and sizes. Two of my favorites are small Santini mums that resemble miniature sunflowers and fresh, green "Kermit" button mums.

DAHLIA Usually available summer to fall in a wide range of sizes and colors. The deep eggplant color is particularly striking.

HYDRANGEA Good for large arrangements; now available all year, although colors vary seasonally.

LILY Available in many colors; the white Casablanca and pink Stargazer have large, fragrant flowers. Lilies will last longer than other flowers as all the buds open.

LISIANTHUS Several large flowers as well as pretty buds growing from one central stem will add height or width to an arrangement.

PEONY The large, dense, round buds open with beautiful soft petals prized for the warm shades from pale pink to coral and burgundy.

ROSE The traditional favorite available in many varieties, including long-stemmed, tea, sweethearts, and spray roses. Garden roses are fragrant but most commercial roses are now bred for color and stem strength, not fragrance. Some of the newer varieties have striped or variegated petals.

SUNFLOWER They make a bold statement with their size and color. Sunflowers look best simply massed in a large jug or combined with other large, colorful flowers.

STOCK Full stems of small fluffy florets in a range of colors from white to deep tones; pastels are a favorite for use in wedding centerpieces.

DAHLIA

PEONY

ROSE

SUNFLOWER

DELICATE FLOWERS

Flowers that have thin or soft stems should be arranged in water. If you are creating your arrangement in wet floral foam, add them last to protect the delicate stems. Most spring flowering bulbs have thick but soft stems that bend or snap easily. Sweet peas have both soft petals and thin stems that require delicate handling. When well conditioned even fragile blooms can last up to a week.

CORNFLOWER Pretty deep-blue or pale pink color, small flower heads on very delicate stems. Use in water or wire to use in summer bouquets or boutonnieres.

DAFFODIL One of the early spring garden flowers, with light yellow "cups" and soft thick stems. Best arranged in water.

LILY OF THE VALLEY Very delicate; easy to grow for spring blooms but expensive as a commercial cut flower. Must be wired for wedding work.

MINIATURE CALLA LILY An expensive, but long lasting and sophisticated accent in wedding bouquets, its thick stem can snap easily. Colors range from soft apricot to rust, pale lavender to deep eggplant, as well as bright yellow and classic white.

RANUNCULUS Has a small multipetal flower head, in vibrant colors, on a soft stem. It needs plenty of water but opens and lasts well.

SWEET PEA Beautiful colors range from white and pastels to deep purple; delicate ruffled petals and extremely thin stems.

TULIP Perfect in a simple clear glass vase, stems can easily snap when inserted in floral foam.

CORNFLOWER

MINIATURE CALLA LILY

RANUNCULUS

SWEET PEA

TALL FLOWERS

There are a number of tall varieties that provide color with clusters of flowers along the length of their stems. These tall flowers add line as well as color and shape to large arrangements. They also make striking displays when used alone. A large vase filled with tall delphinium or larkspur in shades of purple, lavender, and blue makes a strong design statement.

DELPHINIUM A nice range of blue tones, several size variations. The hollow stems need plenty of fresh water; check arrangements daily.

EREMURUS The tall stems of tiny golden flowers bring light into an arrangement. They are expensive but long-lasting.

DELPHINIUM

KANGAROO PAWS This whimsical stem adds tones of yellow, green, orange, or deep red.

LARKSPUR A traditional pastel summer flower; evokes a country-garden feel.

SANDERSONIA Resembles a smaller, more delicate version of Chinese lanterns. Great for autumn arrangements.

KANGAROO PAWS

SNAPDRAGON Very hardy, good range of colors. This is a good choice for a cutting garden.

VIBURNUM Several lacy green balls on a slim woody stem; very graceful. An expensive but charming addition to special-occasion arrangements.

SNAPDRAGON

HYDRANGEA

HYPERICUM BERRIES

MONTE CASINO ASTERS

FILL FLOWERS

I prefer to use fluffy, multiblossomed flowers or stems of berries when fill is needed. The unexpected choice over traditional greenery will make your floral creations unique. Make the best use of readily available seasonal materials to add texture and color.

ASCLEPIAS The bright orange color is perfect for autumn arrangements.

DILL The lacy yellow flowers add texture and fragrance.

HYDRANGEA Extremely adaptable to any occasion; the wide range of colors and sizes makes it a perfect fill or focal flower in all types of arrangements.

HYPERICUM BERRIES The clusters of berries on a sturdy stem are available in delicate peach, crisp green, bright red, and deep burgundy.

MONTE CASINO ASTERS Available year-round in pink, blue, and white; an inexpensive addition for color and height in informal arrangements.

QUEEN ANNE'S LACE The large delicate white flowers add height and lacy fill.

STATICE A traditional fill flower that also dries well for wreaths or other projects.

FOLIAGE

A touch of green intensifies the colors of flowers. Some of my favorites are listed here.

GALAX This round leaf on a single stem is perfect for framing hand-tied bouquets and backing boutonniere flowers.

IVY Can be plucked from the garden as an accent; a traditional greenery used for wedding work.

LEMON LEAF Easy to find, sturdy, and inexpensive; good for wreaths and garlands.

MAGNOLIA LEAF The large, shiny deep-green leaves can also be used on the coppery underside.

SEEDED EUCALYPTUS Beautiful silvery green leaves and clusters of small green berries; use for texture and fill.

MAGNOLIA LEAF

SEEDED EUCALYPTUS

SPECIAL ACCENTS

From late winter through spring take advantage of beautiful flowering branches. They should be arranged in large vases of water to make a dramatic display. The length and shape of branches makes them difficult to combine with cut flowers. To add accents to a centerpiece, clip the branches to short lengths that are easy to handle.

FLOWERING TREES Cherry, apple, pear, quince, and dogwood display clusters of pink or white flowers.

FORSYTHIA The bright yellow flowers on long, slim stems are one of the first signs of spring.

PUSSY WILLOW Soft gray buds add height and texture.

APPLE BLOSSOM

FORSYTHIA

BITTERSWEET

CELOSIA

CHINESE LANTERN

EVERGREEN

In the fall, incorporate materials specific to the season in your designs:

ACORNS Can be wired individually or glued to wooden picks to use in wreaths or floral foam arrangements.

BITTERSWEET Beautiful twisting vines with golden berries that pop open, displaying deep orange seeds. The vines can be cut to add to arrangements or twisted and dried on wreaths.

CELOSIA Choose the plumelike variety or the rich, velvety folds for vibrant color and texture. The flowers are beautiful and unusual but last only several days when cut.

CHINESE LANTERN A traditional autumn favorite for its bright orange color.

SAFFLOWER Golden orange in color with an interesting shape; often used dried.

Winter brings a variety of materials for holiday arrangements:

DOGWOOD BRANCHES Use the red branches for accent or alone in a tall vase.

EVERGREENS Many varieties with different tones and textures: flat cedar, berried blue spruce, and long- or short-needled pine.

HOLLY Beautifully shaped dark-green leaves with red berries; very hardy.

PINECONES They last forever; spray with antique-gold paint for a sophisticated accent.

GARDEN FLOWERS

If you garden, plan on bringing some of your flowers indoors. All of the spring bulb flowers are perfect for cutting to use in simple vase arrangements: tulips, daffodils, narcissus, hyacinth, and grape hyacinth. Summer asters, cosmos, daisies, and zinnias can be cut from the garden and substituted for roses in many floral designs (see Roses on Display, page 76). Try dahlias in place of the golden roses in the Vase arrangement (page 77). Daisies would be a charming substitute for the roses in the Father's Day Gardener's Wreath (page 70).

Color Palettes

Color is one of the most exciting factors in creating ambience with flowers. Using a single color produces a dramatic statement. Different flower types will give depth to a monochromatic palette by adding subtle variations of one color (below). There are some general guidelines for choosing flower colors to convey specific moods.

WHITE AND IVORY   All-white arrangements suit formal occasions. The anniversary party pictured on page 69 combines white flowers with crystal table accessories to set the mood for a stylish celebration.

PINK AND CORAL   From rich, blushing coral to delicate pastels, these warm tones convey happiness and romance—perfect for the Bridal Shower (page 49).

YELLOW   The flowers used in the table runner for the Family Dinner (page 41) contrast fresh yellows with bright green grass for a cheerful celebration of springtime.

ORANGE AND RUST   The depth of autumn tones and textures is beautifully displayed in the Door Swag and Topiary (page 98). As the foliage falls from the trees outside, the warm, inviting colors add a welcome glow to cooler days.

RED   Rich, velvety red flowers are traditional favorites for Christmastime and romantic celebrations. The Winter Wonderland Wedding (page 137) elegantly combines both themes.

BLUE AND PURPLE   These cool tones suggest a relaxed ambience, perfect for a bedside table arrangement.

GREEN   When used alone green conveys a contemporary mood. Consider combining one of the new green roses with green kangaroo paws and viburnum for a very modern bride. The greens used as contrast in the nosegay on page 125 perfectly set off the vibrant flowers for a more traditional look.

Soft, cool colors can make a casual yet very appealing statement, as pictured in the Father's Day Gardener's Wreath on page 71. A few orange roses and dahlias provide just a touch of contrast to intensify the blues and greens. Another of my favorite color combinations is beautifully illustrated by the arrangement on page 133, combining a variety of roses in warm shades with hydrangea. The pink and coral roses are complemented by the tan and red shades of the hydrangea. You will find warm tones are universally appealing and generate a happy feeling that will bring you many compliments on your arrangements.

To coordinate flowers with your room decor match the flower colors to fabrics or pick out a floral motif from a fabric and have fun re-creating it. Experiment with unusual combinations of fresh or dried floral materials to make your creations unique.

floral design basics

D esign basics consist of having the right tools, supplies, and materials and knowing the techniques to use them properly. With a little planning and preparation, it will be easy to create beautiful, long-lasting floral displays.

Taking the time to gather the right materials and supplies for your arrangements will make the process more enjoyable. It is not necessary to have everything listed, but do buy the best floral clippers you can afford. Struggling to cut thick branches with poor quality clippers will turn what should be a fun, creative project into a chore. You should own a sharp knife dedicated to your floral projects. A folding utility knife is a good choice. Your knife and/or clippers will be your most frequently used tools.

The style of container you choose to hold your floral creation is integral to its overall design. Interesting and unusual vases, bowls, bottles, and old china add charm and distinction to arrangements. If you are a collector, consider using baskets, old-fashioned goblets, or enamelware pitchers to add a special touch. Don't worry about chips or slight imperfections: They can easily be hidden by trailing a bit of ivy or positioning a large leaf.

Once you've conditioned the flowers and selected the container, the few simple techniques at the end of this chapter are all you need to know to design displays using the proper mechanics. Master these and you will be filled with confidence and ready to create your own distinctive floral arrangements.

MATERIALS AND SUPPLIES

Containers

BASKETS of all shapes and sizes make excellent floral containers. Be sure to add a waterproof liner unless you are working with dried flowers.

HOUSEHOLD CONTAINERS: footed dishes, urns, teapots, and odd pieces of china or glassware can be turned into unique containers.

VASES: a variety of sizes and shapes in glass, ceramic, pottery, and tin hold blooms of all sizes.

Floral Dishes

SIMPLE PLASTIC DISHES designed to hold wet floral foam setups are available in clear, green, white, and black. They are generally used inside a decorative container but can be used alone if the flowers will cover the dish completely.

Floral Foam

DRY FLORAL FOAM comes in shapes ready-made for many projects: blocks, spheres, cones, topiaries, and wreaths. Most shapes are available in both green and white. You may find the green easier to cover because the color blends with natural materials.

WET FLORAL FOAM (often sold under the brand name Oasis®) is available in a green standard block measuring 9" × 4" × 3". The block can easily be cut to size before or after soaking. There are also many shapes designed for specific uses: wreaths, bouquet holders, and igloos (similar to the top of a bouquet holder without the handle) that can be wired to candelabras or other items.

Finishing Accents

BUTTERFLIES AND LADYBUGS add a whimsical touch to spring and summer arrangements.

GREEN MOSS: green sheet moss can be purchased by the box, moist or dry. There is usually soil clinging to the underside so protect your work surface.

MOSS PINS: use when covering floral foam with moss.

PINS: a selection of sizes with pearl and colored heads will add a special touch to bouquets, corsages, and boutonnieres.

RIBBONS AND RAFFIA: keep a selection of colors and widths to individualize your floral projects.

SPANISH MOSS is often used to hide mechanics.

The Basics

FLOWER FOOD is available in individual packets convenient for home use.

HOT GLUE GUNS (not pictured) are an invaluable tool for working with dried and preserved floral materials. I prefer the low temperature glue guns. Please note—it is very easy to get burned from hot glue. Keep a bowl of cold water nearby. If you do get burned, immediately immerse your finger in cold water to remove the glue and prevent swelling.

NARROW NECKED WATERING CAN (not pictured): use to carefully add water to completed arrangements.

NEEDLE-NOSED PLIERS: use when bending wire into shapes.

ROSE STRIPPER: a handy tool for removing leaves and thorns from sturdy rose stems, this small inexpensive tool is available where floral or garden supplies are sold. To use, hold the rose upright under the head, insert the stem in the small "V" shaped notches at the end of the stripper and gently pull down the stem to strip leaves and thorns. A must when preparing large numbers of roses for wedding work.

SHARP KNIFE: keep a knife dedicated to floral use, I prefer the folding variety. Remember to use and store all sharp tools carefully.

SPRAY BOTTLE OR PLANT MISTER (not pictured): useful for refreshing arrangements made in floral foam.

STEM CLIPPERS: sharp clippers are a must for cutting stems. Clean and dry your clippers after each project.

WATER TUBES are used when you want to place fresh flowers into spaces not large enough for a traditional container.

WIRE CUTTER: an inexpensive pair of wire cutters will be used frequently for straight and spool wire, chenille stems, and chicken wire. Never dull your floral clippers by using them to cut wire.

Tape

CORSAGE TAPE in shades of light and dark green can be matched to flower stems and leaves. It is slightly tacky and will adhere well to floral wire to create a flexible, secure stem for corsage and boutonniere work.

WATERPROOF GREEN FLORAL TAPE secures wet floral foam to its container. The dark green color blends well with the foam. The $1/4$" width is perfect for most jobs. Use the $1/2$" for larger jobs or to finish hand-tied bouquets.

Wire and Fasteners

CHENILLE STEMS in green and white are often preferable to wire when making a bow. The chenille stem is easier on the hands when twisting the tight center.

CHICKEN WIRE is used to add support to floral foam when creating large arrangements. It can also be used to create a grid over the top of a container. The vinyl coated variety is easy on the hands when molding to shape.

WIRE: Straight and spool wire are available in many different gauges; the higher the gauge, the finer the wire. Straight pieces of wire in 18 and 22 gauges are very useful for corsages and boutonnieres. The 22 gauge is commonly used for small flowers and foliage. The 18 gauge is helpful when supporting a rose head. Keep a spool of fine 28-gauge spool wire for delicate stems such as lily of the valley.

WIRED WOOD PICKS: $2 1/2$", 4", and 6" green wood wired picks (they are also available without wire) are used to create stems for irregularly shaped materials. They are useful when adding fruit or vegetables to arrangements in floral foam.

CONDITIONING FLOWERS

When you bring flowers home, strip off all foliage that will be below the water level and cut the stems with a sharp knife or clippers. A diagonal cut will expose a greater portion of the stem's interior so it can take up as much water as possible. Woody stems such as lilac can be gently crushed with a hammer for the same purpose. Thick-stemmed hydrangea responds well to crushing or peeling the end of the stem with a knife. Condition all flowers by giving them a long drink (several hours or overnight in a cool spot out of sunlight) in fresh lukewarm water to which commercial flower food has been added. Flower food is a powder that contains nutrients to help cut flowers last longer.

There are also products to help flowers take up water quickly. This is very useful for hydrangea, where the large heads of soft florets need a good supply of water to stay fresh. Mix a small amount of the liquid with water, as directed on the bottle, and quickly dip the stems in the solution before placing them in the conditioning bucket. Check with your local floral supplier for available products.

MECHANICS AND TECHNIQUES

When beginning any floral project, read the directions completely from beginning to end. Assemble your tools and materials on a clean tabletop or other work surface. Newspaper or plastic will protect the work area and make clean-up quick and easy. Allow adequate time to complete the design. The simplest arrangements can take as little as twenty minutes while more complex designs can take an hour or more to complete.

There are many "invisible aids" that will provide the mechanics to support your arrangement, regardless of its size. Study the following techniques to decide if tape, chicken wire, or floral foam is the best choice for the size of your container and the height of your flowers.

Arranging Flowers in Water

There are three ways to arrange flowers in water. The first is by using a tape grid. A round rose bowl (also called a bubble bowl) is perfect for this method. Start with a clean, dry container and use $^1/_4$"-wide waterproof floral tape to make a grid across the top. The tape should extend just beyond the lip of the container. When the grid is complete run a strip of tape around the top edge. Fill the bowl with water and arrange your flowers. Be sure to cascade flowers or leaves over the edge to cover the tape.

TAPE GRID

Another aid to arranging in water is a chicken wire grid. This method is more frequently used with opaque containers, and is an excellent way to support tall flowers. Cut a piece of chicken wire slightly wider than the opening of the container. Bend the edges under and mold to fit the opening. If you don't have the vinyl-coated variety, protect your hands with gloves or use pliers when bending the wire. If your arrangement will be full and cascading, make a round cage of chicken wire to extend above the container.

CHICKEN WIRE GRID

The third way to arrange flowers in water is by making a hand-tied bouquet. This gives a very clean look and is desirable when using glass or a delicate or expensive vase that might be marred by tape or chicken wire. It also works well for very small vases. You may have to practice several times to create a round, balanced arrangement. Mix the sizes and textures of flowers so that the smaller or cluster-type flowers fill the spaces between the larger single stem flowers. Secure the stems of the completed bouquet with $^1/_2$" waterproof floral tape and clip stems. For a professional finish wrap the stems with a flat leaf and secure with a pin.

HAND-TIED BOUQUET

Arranging Flowers in Floral Foam

Wet floral foam is very easy to work with. Available in 9" × 4" × 3" blocks as well as premade shapes such as wreaths and bouquet holders, it can be easily cut to fit any container, holds stems firmly in place, and, if kept moist, will keep arrangements fresh up to one week. Before using, cut the foam to the size and shape of the container and thoroughly soak it in a sink or bucket of lukewarm water. When the foam is fully saturated it will sink. Secure the soaked foam to the dish or container with waterproof floral tape. This is referred to as a floral setup. Setups can also be made in advance using plastic dishes; just soak the whole setup as needed. Use a plastic liner to hold the foam if your container is not watertight or is fragile. The foam should extend above the rim of the container. This will allow room for floral elements to cascade gracefully over the edges. If you should reposition flowers while arranging, do not insert a stem into an existing hole, as an air pocket will develop and the flower will not be able to take in water.

FLORAL FOAM SETUPS

Very large arrangements or those using heavy materials require the use of chicken wire over the saturated foam. Be sure the depth of the foam will accommodate one-third to one-half of the stem length. Taped securely, the setup will safely support tall or heavy materials.

USING WOOD PICKS

Wood picks are an excellent tool for adding heavy or irregular, stemless materials to arrangements in foam. Unwired picks can be hot-glued to pinecones or inserted directly into fruits and vegetables. To cascade grapes or berries over the edge of a dish, use a wired pick.

Bridal Flowers

Extra time spent designing wedding flowers is always well worth the effort. Seeing your floral designs admired the day of the wedding, and captured forever in photographs, will bring immense satisfaction. Always use the best quality flowers and give plenty of attention to all the special details.

Before starting a hand-tied bouquet of any size, remove the foliage from the stems and separate the flowers by type. It will be much easier to work if you can clearly see the variety and quantity of your materials. Start the bouquet with a central flower and add stems at a slight angle, working in a circle. Vary the materials for interest. When you have reached the desired size, secure the stems with waterproof tape.

A well-balanced hand-tied bouquet will stand without support. If the bouquet is for a vase, simply cut the stems and insert. If you are making a bridal bouquet, make a collar with leaves or other material and tape the stems securely. Wrap the stems with ribbon and secure with decorative pearl pins.

BOUQUET HOLDERS

Foam-filled bouquet holders are an excellent choice if the bouquet needs to remain fresh from a morning ceremony through an evening reception. They are available in several sizes; the largest is usually used for the bride's bouquet and the smaller ones for her attendants' flowers.

Start by using fresh, well-conditioned flowers. Add the largest blooms first and work all around the foam in the holder to create a nicely rounded shape with levels of interest. Add small foliage and flowers to fill out the back. Wrap the plastic handle with ribbon, securing with hot glue. Fluffy bows of sheer ribbon will hide all traces of the plastic holder. Small buds and leaves tied into ribbons make decorative floral streamers.

WIRING WEDDING FLOWERS

Delicate ferns and flowers should be wired with fine 28-gauge spool wire, being careful not to snap the stems.

Wire leaves by creating a "U" shape to support the underside. Twist the wire together and tape over the new stem.

Full but soft ranunculus need a 22-gauge wire inserted into the flower head. A small hook formed at the top will be buried as the wire is gently pulled down, but not completely through, the flower.

When preparing clusters of berries, make sure the wire goes above the center stem to stabilize the cluster.

Heavy flowers such as rose heads and carnations should be wired by pushing one wire up into the base of the flower using a 6" length of 18 gauge wire for large roses and 22-gauge for smaller flowers. Add a second wire, perpendicular to the first, piercing the base of the flower. Bend the second wire to meet the first wire. You will now have 3 pieces of wire to twist together and cover with corsage tape.

CORSAGES AND BOUTONNIERES

Long-lasting roses are a classic choice for wedding flowers. The range of sizes and colors makes them suitable for any style of celebration. For example, a corsage of beautiful roses with matching sheer ribbon makes a stunning choice for female relatives of the bride and groom.

A classic rose boutonniere can be individualized in many ways: accented with ivy and berries or soft astilbe and a few tiny thistles, fanned with leaves, or use a long narrow leaf for a dramatic effect. The stems can be simply clipped and wrapped with corsage tape or ribbon, curled into a tendril, or twisted with copper wire.

MAKING BOWS

A five-loop bow is the basic bow used for floral design. Use delicate sheer ribbon for a corsage, rich double-faced satin ribbon for a bride's bouquet, and a rustic woven ribbon for an autumn wreath. Hold the ribbon between your thumb and first finger. Make a loop and twist the ribbon as you secure it under your thumb to make the next loop. The two outer loops should be the longest. The center loop is the smallest. Vary the number of loops to make a larger or smaller bow. Pinch the finished bow in the center and secure tightly with wire or a chenille stem.

spring

Spring bulbs bloom early in the season

with tender green buds and fresh color, hinting at the display to come.

Golden yellow daffodils, blue-violet grape hyacinth, and regal tulips

in every hue imaginable bring color to the home and garden.

These flowers last very well, with tight buds opening to full flower.

Just display in plenty of water and remember

they prefer cooler temperatures.

WHITE
apple blossom
dogwood
hyacinth
hydrangea
lilac
lily of the valley
narcissus
stock
tulip

YELLOW
daffodil
forsythia
freesia
pansy
ranunculus
stock
tulip

RED
ranunculus
rose
tulip

PINK
cherry blossom
dogwood
hyacinth
hydrangea
rose
tulip

CORAL / PEACH
quince
rose
stock
tulip

LAVENDER / PURPLE
freesia
hyacinth
iris
lilac
stock
tulip
violet

BLUE
forget-me-not
grape hyacinth
hydrangea

Engagement Dinner

Cool blues and greens accent creamy peach roses to create the soft color palette for this very special occasion. Green grapes and kumquats echo the floral colors and add texture to the mix, while an abundance of votive candles cast a warm, romantic glow over the table. Rather than the usual large centerpiece, this design groups three floral dishes with small round glass vases. At each place setting a vase provides the guest with a take-home remembrance of an evening shared with close friends.

The peach ribbon tied to each napkin adds special detail to the decor.

flowers & fruit

10 small bunches green grapes

12 stems light blue or lavender hydrangea

10 stems green hydrangea

12 stems white lilac

12 stems Sahara roses

22 stems peach roses

20 stems white spray roses

30 stems grape hyacinth

10 stems green viburnum

20–30 kumquats

supplies

3 low footed floral bowls 6"–8" in diameter

1 1/2 blocks floral foam

1/4" waterproof floral tape

4" wired wood picks

9 yards white wired ribbon 3/4" wide for arrangements

3/4" peach wired ribbon to tie napkins (26" per napkin)

6–8 round glass vases 2 1/2" in diameter (one for each place setting)

8–10 round glass votive cups

8–10 tea lights

1. Prepare floral setups in footed bowls. Use one-half block of soaked foam for each.

2. Attach wired floral picks to 6 bunches of grapes. Secure 2 bunches in each setup, cascading over the side (figure 1).

figure 1

3. Cut hydrangea and place 5 stems (3 blue, 2 green) in setup to create a low, rounded shape (figure 2). Add 3 stems of lilac to each. Add roses in multicolored clusters grouping 3–5 roses for a very full arrangement. Tuck in 4–6 stems of grape hyacinth and 3 stems green viburnum for color.

figure 2

4. Cut white ribbon into 36" lengths. Make nine 3-loop bows with streamers (page 33) and secure to wired picks. Position 3 bows in floral foam for each arrangement.

5. Use a small piece of hydrangea, several roses, viburnum, and touches of grape hyacinth to make a hand-tied nosegay for each small vase.

❋ flower style

Buy inexpensive glass votive holders in quantity to save money. You can also use them as miniature vases.

6. Cluster the 3 footed bowls in the center of the table. See the diagram (figure 3) for placement. Arrange remaining bunches of grapes and kumquats around the bases of the bowls. Position a small vase near each place setting and scatter the votive candles throughout the elements of the centerpiece.

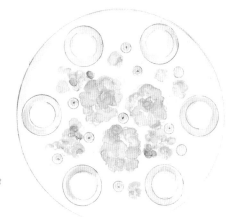

figure 3

Family Supper

A runner of fresh grass makes a whimsical base for the first flowers and vegetables of spring. Delicate flowers contrast with the more substantial vegetables, hollowed out to form unique containers. The sunny outdoor theme is continued with the napkin nosegays of miniature vegetables. A natural place-card holder is made by cutting a slit in a small fruit.

flowers & vegetables

1 tray wheat grass (approximately 12" × 18")

7–9 small vegetables: white eggplants, yellow and green peppers

20 stems yellow sweet pea

10 stems lily of the valley

10 stems orange ranunculus

10 stems yellow pansies

5 stems yellow miniature calla lilies

sprigs of parsley, rosemary, oregano, or other herbs

miniature vegetables for accents and napkin treatments: carrots, yellow squash, zucchini, grape tomatoes

limes for place-card holders

supplies

clear cellophane or waxed paper

white-headed pins

5 yards pale yellow or white acetate ribbon 1 1/2" wide

18-gauge floral wire

corsage tape

flower style

This design could be reworked in many ways. In the fall, try mini pumpkins and squash filled with gold and rust mums nestled in a runner of soft green moss. Tuck in votive candles for an evening party. Use citrus fruit, pineapples and papayas for a mid-summer tropical theme.

1. Take the wheat grass out of the tray and cut it lengthwise into 3 strips. Use a sharp knife to cut through the roots and soil.

2. Protect the center of the table with a strip of cellophane and position the wheat grass to form the runner. Trim the cellophane and pin ribbon at base of grass to hide the soil (figure 1).

figure 1

3. Using a small, sharp knife, hollow out the peppers and eggplants to use as floral containers (figure 2). For peppers: Cut a slice off the top and remove the seeds and membranes. Fill half full with water. For eggplants: Cut a thin slice from the bottom so the eggplant stands. Hollow out a small area in the top 2" deep and fill with water.

figure 2

4. As pictured in the photograph, make small, loose hand-tied nosegays of single flower types with herb accents. Cut the stems short and place in the vegetable containers.

5. Distribute the floral and vegetable pieces along the length of the grass runner. Add clusters of small vegetables for additional color.

6. For each napkin decoration, wire 3 miniature vegetables and bind together with corsage tape. Twist around napkin and twirl ends to form a tendril (figure 3). Tuck in a single flower head.

figure 3

7. Cut a small slit in each lime and insert place cards.

Fragrance in the Home

This extravagant display bursts with the heady fragrance of roses and lilacs. The beautiful pink tones are enhanced by the additional rose heads and petals that fill the glass vase. Although it looks dramatic, this arrangement is relatively easy to make. Use garden or purchased flowers and vary the colors by season. To keep the arrangement fresh, be sure to change the water every other day.

flowers

10 stems white lilac

10 stems pale pink stock

15 stems perfect pink and/or peach roses

20 matching rose heads for vase

supplies

1/4" waterproof floral tape

glass vase (al least 8" tall and 6" wide)

1. Make a loose bouquet using most of the lilac, stock and roses (figure 1). Put a few flowers aside for filling out the completed arrangement.

2. Tape the bouquet stems and place into the vase half full of water (figure 2).

figure 1

figure 2

3. Carefully push the rose heads into the water to hide the bouquet stems (figure 3).

4. Gently position the remaining flowers to fill out the bouquet, making sure to place the stems into the center of the vase so they will be hidden by rose heads. Submerge any petals or broken flowers and add water to fill the vase.

figure 3

✳ flower style

Materials below the water level in an arrangement will rot if not handled properly. Make sure stems are stripped of their leaves before arranging. To keep the water and submerged flowers of this arrangement fresh, add flower food or a few drops of household bleach to the water and place the arrangement away from direct sunlight. Be sure to handle the vase very carefully when changing the water.

Mother's Day

Slip a hand-tied bouquet into a pretty cone holder and present it to mom or grand-mother on her day. These pressed tin cones are designed to be hung on a door, cabinet, or in a window. Smaller versions can be made from beautiful handmade papers—just be sure to add watertight liners. If desired, you could substitute a rustic twig basket in a similar shape. This is a great project in which to involve children. They can choose the flower colors, decorate paper for cones, or tie ribbons.

flowers

(quantities may need to be adjusted for cone size)

BOUQUET #1

20 stems white narcissus

BOUQUET #2

12 stems yellow narcissus

8 stems white ranunculus

3 stems white freesia

BOUQUET #3

6 stems white ranunculus

3 stems white phlox

15–20 stems lily of the valley with leaves

BOUQUET #4

3 stems lavender roses (save a few leaves)

3 stems white phlox

6 stems white veronica

8 stems lavender sweet peas

supplies

cones or wall pocket baskets with liners

ribbon for hanging (if needed)

1/4" waterproof floral tape

1. Prepare cones with ribbons and liners; add a small amount of water. Sort flowers by type.

2. Make a small nosegay for each cone, starting with flowers that will be in the center. Add the remaining flowers to create a well-balanced, round shape.

3. Secure the nosegay with waterproof floral tape. Clip stems before placing in water (figure 1).

figure 1

Bridal Shower

When female friends and relatives gather to celebrate an upcoming marriage, it is time to decorate with a feminine hand. Instead of a large, elaborate centerpiece, showcase special floral combinations in a number of smaller holders. Bring out your favorite containers—silver julep cups, delicate tea cups, pressed-glass vases, teapots, or water pitchers. Use pretty spring colors to make each bouquet one-of-a-kind. Extravagant peonies and lilacs, delicate freesia, ranunculus surrounded by fragrant lilacs, and ruffled sweet peas are just the start. For the bride, a trio of all white fragrant flowers such as lilacs, paperwhites, and lilies of the valley are perfect.

flowers

(not all flowers listed are pictured)

PINK: ranunculus, spray roses, tulips

LAVENDER: anenomes, freesia, lilacs, sweet peas, veronica

PEACH/CHAMPAGNE: roses, stock

WHITE: lilacs, lilies of the valley, narcissus, ranunculus, roses

supplies

variety of unique, watertight containers

1. Select flowers for each container.

2. Starting with the center flowers, make a loose hand-tied nosegay to fit each container.

3. Clip the stem ends and gently place the nosegays in the water-filled containers. These nosegays are not taped, which allows the flowers to relax to the shape of the containers.

🐝 flower style

It is much easier to make a small bouquet from small flowers. If you want to add a few larger roses, be sure to have a soft multiblossomed flower like lilac or phlox to fill in the spaces between the larger flower heads.

Spring Afternoon Wedding

This inviting springtime decor is designed for a small wedding on a late afternoon. Warm coral and peach flowers are set off by light green viburnum, and the buffet menu coordinates with the color scheme. Silver table accessories provide a touch of elegance, while candlelight adds a romantic glow to the sunset-timed cake cutting.

Bride's Bouquet

Personal flowers require a skilled hand and attention to detail. For the bride's lace-bordered bouquet, only roses of the palest hues accented with traditional stephanotis and lilies of the valley are used.

flowers

10 stems cream roses

8 stems pale peach roses

5 stems champagne sweetheart roses

3–4 stems white lilac, all greens removed

10 white stephanotis flowers

25 stems lily of the valley

15 galax leaves

supplies

28-gauge floral spool wire

small floral foam bouquet holder

lace-trimmed cone to fit back of holder
(these come commercially prepared with
lace or you can add your own trim)

10 premade white stephanotis stems

hot glue gun

1. Remove all foliage from rose and lilac stems and place in water. Let the flowers drink in a cool place several hours or overnight.

2. Dip the cotton end of the stephanotis stems in water and insert them into the center of the stephanotis flowers (figure 1).

figure 1

3. Carefully wire the stems of the lily of the valley using fine-gauge wire (figure 2).

figure 2

4. Cut the rose stems to varying lengths from 2" to 5" and insert them into the floral foam, working around the foam to create a balanced round shape.

5. Tuck springs of lilac between the roses. The tips of the lilac should extend above the roses. Add the stephanotis, clipping the stems as needed.

6. To finish, insert the delicate stems of lily of the valley. This is a dense bouquet but the lilac and lily of the valley keep it from being stiff. Collar the bouquet with galax leaves.

7. Slip the bouquet holder into the lace-trimmed cone. Wrap the handle with ribbon, securing at the top and bottom with a dot of hot glue. Cover any exposed plastic on the back with leaves or bows.

Groom's Boutonniere

The champagne sweetheart roses used in the bride's bouquet are repeated in this charming boutonniere.

flowers

2 stems champagne sweetheart roses
   with leaves

supplies

18- and 22-gauge straight wires

light green corsage tape

1. Wire the roses with 18-gauge wire (page 32) and tape stems to 4" long.

2. Select three perfect rose leaves and wire with 22-gauge wire. Cut wires to 1" and tape stems.

3. Twist all stems together and cover with corsage tape to make a smooth single stem about 3"– 4" long. Twist around a pencil to form a tendril and add a pin for securing to lapel.

Flower Girl's Basket

An assortment of contrasting pale and bright roses fill this pretty basket.

flowers

8 stems coral roses

10 peach single-stem or spray roses

12 stems tiny coral Serena roses

10 stems Queen Anne's lace

supplies

small basket with plastic liner

1 block floral foam, cut to basket shape

1/4" waterproof floral tape

1/2 yard white tulle

2 white chenille stems

1. Prepare floral setup in basket liner (figure 1).

figure 1

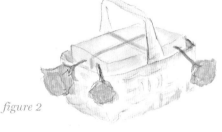

figure 2

2. Cut large rose stems to varying lengths from 5" to 7" and insert them into the soaked foam, keeping the flowers at slightly different heights and evenly distributing the colors (figure 2). Add the miniature roses.

3. Fill in spaces with Queen Anne's lace.

4. Cut two strips of tulle 6" × 24" to make 2 fluffy bows. Secure the bows with chenille stems and attach to the basket handles (photo, page 56).

Mother of the Bride's Corsage

flowers

1 perfect peach rose

1 stem heather, cut into small pieces

pieces of small-leaved greenery such as
   boxwood or pittosporum

1 stem fern

supplies

18-gauge straight wire

28-gauge spool wire

light green corsage tape

1/2 yard ivory ribbon 1/2" wide

1 lace handkerchief

2–3 pearl-headed corsage pins

1. Wire the rose and stronger stemmed materials with the 18-gauge wire.
   Use the 28-gauge spool wire for the delicate fern.

2. Wrap all wire stems with corsage tape.

3. Using the rose as the center flower, add the other
   floral materials, twisting the wire stems together as
   each is added (figure 1). Make sure a sprig or two of
   greenery is facing down to hide the mechanics.

figure 1

4. Make a bow (page 33) and secure it to the corsage
   stem with spool wire.

5. Bind all wires with corsage tape and trim neatly.

6. Gather the handkerchief from the middle and pin
   it to clothing (figure 2). Position corsage on top
   and secure with additional pins.

figure 2

Buffet Centerpiece

flowers

6 stems white larkspur

10 stems green viburnum

10 stems white lilac

10 stems Queen Anne's lace

10 stems peach roses

10 stems coral ranunculus

supplies

10"–12"-tall glass vase

¹/₄" waterproof floral tape

1. Prepare the vase with a tape grid (page 27).

2. Use white larkspur and the tallest pieces of viburnum, lilac, and Queen Anne's lace to outline the top and side dimensions of the arrangement (figure 1).

3. Use the photo as a guide to place the roses and ranunculus. Work around the front and sides of the vase. (This arrangement is designed to be seen three-quarters of the way around. If you would like the arrangement to be seen from all sides, add about one-fourth more flowers and work all around the vase.)

4. Add the remaining lilacs and viburnum where fill is needed and to cascade over the edge of the vase.

5. Finish with more Queen Anne's lace for a light, airy feel.

figure 1

summer

The warm sunny summer is the time to use bright colorful blooms.
Combine tall garden flowers with shorter varieties as they appear in nature.
Take advantage of the summer's bounty by adding fruits and vegetables
to your arrangements. When designing with flowers from your own garden,
cut them early in the day when they will be at their freshest.

WHITE
bellflower
larkspur
peony
phlox
snapdragon
sweet pea
veronica

LAVENDER / PURPLE
allium
delphinium
larkspur
scabious
snapdragon
sweet pea
veronica

CORAL / PEACH / ORANGE
cosmos
lily
rose
snapdragon
sweet pea
yarrow
zinnia

YELLOW
cosmos
dill
eremurus
miniature calla lily
snapdragon
sunflower

BLUE
ageratum
cornflower
delphinium
hydrangea
Monte Casino aster

PINK/RED
astilbe
foxglove
godetia
peony
phlox
snapdragon
sweet William

Saturday Night Buffet

Pull out all the stops for an elegant summer dinner party. Time your guests' arrival for just before sundown to integrate the vibrant outdoor colors with the lush table decor. A variety of flowers are used to make this striking buffet centerpiece. Green viburnum and bunches of grapes cool the punch of hot color provided by the roses, calla lilies, and ranunculus. Graceful, curving golden yellow eremurus adds height. Fruits and vegetables, spilling from the arrangement, are surprise elements that add a note of originality to the tabletop. The combination of bright colors and natural materials creates a very sophisticated table celebrating summer.

flowers, fruits, & vegetables

5 stems yellow eremurus

10 stems green viburnum

8 stems yellow and/or hot pink roses

6 stems mango-colored calla lily

20 stems hot pink and/or orange ranunculus

8 stems small black-eyed Susan

10–12 artichokes, small and large

5 blood oranges

6 bunches green grapes

3 green apples

supplies

Container (the container shown is a rusted-iron footed urn)

Dish for container (if not watertight)

floral foam

chicken wire

1/2" waterproof floral tape

4" wired wood picks

6" unwired wood picks

1. Prepare fruits and vegetables for the arrangement (figure 1). Pierce 8 artichoke stems with 6" picks. Cut one section from each blood orange. Pierce oranges and removed sections with wood picks. Secure several bunches of grapes to 4" wired picks.

figure 1

2. Prepare the container or dish with a setup of soaked floral foam and chicken wire (page 00). The height and weight of the materials require chicken wire for support. Add the eremurus and viburnum first, to establish the height of the arrangement; then add the large artichokes, sectioned oranges, and grapes on picks, keeping the larger items low in the arrangement because of their weight (figure 2).

figure 2

3. Add the roses, evenly distributing colors. Position the calla lilies to peek above the roses. Add the orange sections. Gently place the ranunculus to add color where needed.

4. Use the black-eyed Susan to make sure that the foam setup is totally covered by floral materials.

5. Position the apples and remaining grapes, artichokes, and flower heads on the tabletop, around the base of the container.

Birthday Luncheon

The fragrance and color of a summer garden set the scene for a festive birthday. Flowers are everywhere—cubes of fresh fruit are skewered on stems of lavender and nasturtiums brighten savory sandwiches. The napkin treatment, tied with raffia and fresh herbs, shows special attention to details. The focal point of the table is a simple galvanized bucket crowned with a bright array of traditional summer flowers. Note how the yarrow and chamomile flowers add soft fullness low in the arrangement to balance the tall stems of larkspur and snapdragons.

flowers

3 stems tall pink larkspur or garden phlox

6 stems pink or yellow snapdragon

3 stems pink foxglove

5 stems yellow yarrow

5 stems pink yarrow

7 stems chamomile flowers (or Monte Casino asters)

5 stems deep pink dianthus

5 stems purple pansies

herbs, stems of lavender, and flowers from the garden for fruit skewers and napkins

nasturtiums for the sandwich tray

supplies

chicken wire cut slightly larger than the opening of the bucket

galvanized bucket or pitcher

natural raffia

1. Fill the bucket two-thirds full with water. Bend the edges of the chicken wire and position it about 1" below the opening of the bucket (page 27).

2. Cut the stems of the tallest flowers (larkspur, snapdragons, foxglove) to about one-and-a-half times the height of the container. The chicken wire will hold the tall flowers in the center of the bucket. This will give you plenty of room to create an abundant arrangement.

3. Add the fuller flowers (yarrow, chamomile) in clusters for width. Place them lower to spill over the edge of the container. Remember to cut flower stems to different lengths for a natural look.

4. Add the stems of dianthus and pansies last.

5. Decorate the sandwiches with nasturtiums.

6. Tie the napkins with raffia and insert a sprig of herb and several small flowers.

❋ flower style

Use care when selecting blooms for decoration and consumption. Any flowers used in or near food should be pesticide free. If you are in doubt, don't use the flowers. Edible flowers are often sold in gourmet shops. You will find small containers in the refrigerated section near the fruits or vegetables. Most often found are nasturtiums and pansies, used to give accents of bright color to green salad; and violet blossoms, perfect for decorating special desserts.

Happy Anniversary

This beautiful table, set for a special anniversary, evokes memories of a June wedding. Flowers can be as simple as those pictured or as elaborate as your skills and budget allow. A few perfect garden blooms can be as lovely as professionally arranged flowers.

flowers

(adjust quantities to fit your vases)

10 stems white spray roses

10 stems white ranunculus

5 stems light blue delphinium

5 stems white phlox (or other cluster type flowers like stock or hyacinth)

5 stems star of Bethlehem

1 box stephanotis

supplies

6 small glass vases

1 glass vase about 6" tall

1. Trim leaves from all stems for a very clean look.

2. Cut spray roses, ranunculus, and delphinium to make small bunches. Trim stems to fit in small vases.

3. Group white phlox and star of Bethlehem and trim stems to fit in the taller glass vase.

4. Arrange stephanotis and delphinium florets around and on top of the cake (figure 1).

figure 1

Father's Day Gardener's Wreath

Crown your Father's Day table with a wreath designed to express your appreciation for dad's hard work in the garden. The charm of this project is in combining the natural materials on the wreath with miniature potted plants. The flowers include hydrangea, roses, heather, and dahlias with soft light green foliage. If you are making this for an evening gathering tuck a few candles into the wreath or drop tea lights into tiny terra-cotta flowerpots for rustic votives.

flowers

one 3" pot heather

10 stems light blue hydrangea, plus leaves

6 stems orange roses

12 stems orange dahlias or zinnias

2 or 3 stems white Monte Casino asters

one 3"–4" pot rosemary

cuttings of dusty miller, silver sage, ageratum, marigolds, button mums, berries, or other small summer plants

supplies

12" floral foam wreath

four 3"-tall candles

4" wired wood floral picks

2" miniature terra-cotta flower pots

small pieces of floral foam

1. Soak the wreath form in water.

2. Press the pot of heather gently on the wreath to make an indentation. Use the mark to cut a circle from the wet foam about half as deep as the pot. Press the potted heather plant firmly into the foam (figure 1).

figure 1

3. Position candles, press into foam to hold firmly in place (figure 2).

figure 2

4. Break up large hydrangea heads into 3 or 4 pieces each. Use wired picks to reinforce the stems (figure 3). Insert hydrangea to fill out the shape of the wreath.

5. Add splashes of color with clusters of roses and dahlias. Cut asters in short pieces and insert into wreath.

figure 3

6. Add bits of dusty miller or other foliage to extend from the wreath and make the shape more natural looking. Fill any spaces with hydrangea leaves.

7. Fill the miniature terra-cotta flower pots with bits of soaked floral foam and flowers or small plants and place in center of wreath.

8. Place pot of rosemary at an angle in the center of the completed wreath.

⚘ flower style

For an extra-special treat, accent this wreath with miniature garden accessories: tools, watering cans, and baskets. You could also add a few artificial butterflies or lady bugs.

Creative Camouflage

This imaginative arrangement makes a very dramatic statement. The seeded eucalyptus covering the container offers soft shades of green as well as texture from the leaves and berries, extending upward into the flowers. The charm of this display is that the container and flowers have become one natural unit.

flowers

10–15 stems flat-leaf eucalyptus with berries

5 stems small blue thistle

4 stems purple statice

5 stems deep red hypericum berries

4 stems white Monte Casino asters

15 stems coral crown asters

6 stems bright yellow roses

10 stems orange crocosmia

supplies

¹/₄" waterproof floral tape

12"–16"-tall container (a plastic vase or galvanized bucket)

hot-glue gun

18-gauge green spool wire

natural raffia

1. Make a tape grid on top of container (page 27).

2. Lay the container on its side and position a few pieces of eucalyptus; secure with hot glue and wrap with spool wire (figure 1).

figure 1

3. Continue working in sections (figure 2) until entire container is covered. Tie with a thick bundle of raffia (figure 3). Trim ends.

figure 2

figure 3

4. Use the remaining eucalyptus to start the arrangement (figure 4). Add the thistles, statice, hypericum berries, and Monte Casino asters to create a tall, full shape.

5. Cluster the coral asters and add the yellow roses.

6. Finish with the crocosmia for an airy touch of deep orange.

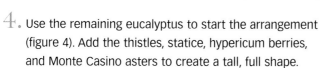

figure 4

Roses on Display

These two arrangements illustrate the endless versatility of roses. Sunset Bouquet is all about contrasts, with large yellow roses framed by deep purple and bright orange flowers. The variety of colors, shapes and textures soften the stern lines and somber colors of the antique furnishings. Pink Extravaganza bursts with a lavish display of loosely arranged, feminine pink roses. Set on a crisp white linen tablecloth, it makes a lovely centerpiece for an outdoor tea party.

Sunset Bouquet

flowers

10 stems orange snapdragons

3 stems orange roses

10 stems golden yellow roses

5 stems purple globe thistle

10 stems lavender

3 stems purple lisianthus

several large rounded leaves (from the garden or purchased galax leaves)

supplies

vase

1/4" waterproof floral tape

1. Make a tape grid on the vase (page 27); add water.

2. Add snapdragons first to create a fan-shaped outline for the arrangement.

3. Fill in with roses. Add the globe thistle and lavender to create levels.

4. Insert the lisianthus to intensify the rich tones of purple. Tuck in a few large, rounded leaves to cover the top of the vase.

Pink Extravaganza

flowers

30–35 stems fully open single-stem and spray
    roses: light pink, deep pink,
    variegated pink, creamy white

3 or 4 stems green hydrangea

3–5 stems deep purple statice

supplies

large oval decorative bowl

floral foam

1/4" waterproof floral tape

figure 1

1. Place cut soaked floral foam in bowl to extend over top. Tape to hold firmly in place (figure 1).

2. Arrange flowers in a low, loose style, alternating contrasting flower colors to show off the blooms (figure 2).

3. Scatter a few rose heads and petals on the table for a casual yet opulent effect.

figure 2

✿ flower style

If you enjoy gardening, try growing different varieties of roses to use in your arrangements. When buying roses, explore all the options available to you. Cut roses can be purchased at floral shops, local green markets, or by mail.

Summer Garden Wedding

This cheerful decor for a summer wedding at home provides a charming setting for a celebration with family and close friends. Bright colors and collections of antique tableware reflect the personal style of the bride and groom.

Bride's Bouquet

This lovely grouping of pastel flowers was designed in a bouquet holder to keep the flowers hydrated on a warm summer day.

flowers

4 stems light blue hydrangea

12 stems yellow roses

15 stems scabious with buds (assorted lavender, light blue, and white)

3 stems white bellflower

3 stems white Monte Casino aster

supplies

large floral foam bouquet holder

4" wired wood picks

1 yard white satin ribbon $3/4$" wide

3 yards white sheer ribbon $3/4$" wide

hot-glue gun

1. Remove foliage from all flower stems and separate the flowers by type. Place the flowers in containers of cool water and allow them to drink several hours or overnight. It is much easier to design a bouquet with your flowers sorted and ready to use.

2. Start the bouquet with hydrangea and roses working all around the holder. The largest flowers will create the size of the bouquet (page 31).

3. Add the scabious, reinforcing or lengthening the stems as needed with wired picks. Cut the long stems of bellflower into 3 or 4 short pieces. These flowers should peek above the hydrangea. Complete the bouquet with clusters of Monte Casino asters to fill as needed.

4. Cover the plastic bouquet handle with satin ribbon, securing with a dot of hot glue at the bottom. Overlapping the ribbon, wrap tightly to the top. Fold under and dot with glue.

5. The back of the bouquet holder can be covered with bows. Make 4 small bows using 12" of sheer ribbon for each. Attach the bows to wired picks and insert into the small holes in the back of the holder (page 31).

6. For a playful touch, tie small buds into 10"–18" lengths of sheer ribbon and attach to a wired pick. Insert the pick into the foam to create flowing streamers for the bouquet.

✿ flower style

If you have never worked with an Oasis® bouquet holder, buy several and practice with inexpensive flowers. Always add the hardiest flowers first and the most delicate last so they won't get crushed as you work.

Groom's Boutonniere

This classic rose boutonniere will stay fresh on a warm day.

flowers

1 stem yellow rose

3 stems scabious buds

materials

18-gauge straight wire

28-gauge spool wire

light green floral tape

6" piece of $3/8$" wide white satin ribbon

6" piece of $3/8$" wide white sheer ribbon

2 straight pins

boutonniere pin

1. Cut the rose stem and prepare with straight wire (page 32).

2. Wire the scabious buds with spool wire, inserting one end into the underside of the bud. Twist wire around the stems and cover with tape.

3. Cover all wires with tape and twist together.

4. Cut stems to about 2" and wrap with satin ribbon, securing at each end with a straight pin pushed lengthwise into stems. Tie the sheer ribbon in a simple square knot and add a pin for securing to lapel (photo, page 80).

Three-tiered Arrangement

This buffet arrangement brings together a delightful array of summer flowers. The graduated galvanized containers match larger ones used to cool the champagne and the three levels echo the tiers of the wedding cake.

flowers

3 stems blue delphinium

5 stems blue hydrangea

3 stems orange tulips

3 stems miniature sunflowers

8 stems purple ageratum

5 stems pink phlox

8 stems dill flowers

6 stems lavender veronica

3 stems pink dahlias

8 stems yellow nasturtium

3 stems purple statice

3 stems red sweet William

3 stems light blue scabious

8 stems burgundy miniature carnations

3 stems yellow roses

6 stems dusty miller

4 pieces ivy

supplies

3 galvanized buckets in graduated sizes
(the largest should be about
10"–12" in diameter)

floral foam to fill each

utility knife

1. Tightly pack each container with soaked floral foam, extending the foam about 2" above the rim.

2. Place the middle container on the large container and gently press it into the foam. Cut a shallow circle about $1/2$" deep from the foam in the large container. Firmly press the middle container into the foam of the large container (figure 1).

figure 1

3. Working outward from the foam so flowers cascade gracefully over the edges (figure 2), distribute the flower types and colors throughout the 3 tiers, beginning at the bottom and inserting the larger flowers first. The completed arrangement should have a casual garden look.

4. Because this arrangement is displayed outdoors on a warm day, keep the foam moist and mist the completed arrangement well to keep it fresh.

figure 2

✳ flower style

Flowers can be used in a number of ways to decorate the buffet table. Colorful and long-lasting flower heads such as nasturtiums or crown asters can be easily secured around the edge of a table to add a colorful floral border on a crisp white tablecloth. Use straight pins to keep the flowers in place, working from under the tablecloth to hide the pins.

Arrange fresh fruit in pretty tiered dishes and tuck flowers in the layers. Hydrangea will stay fresh if stems are inserted in water tubes.

autumn

The flowers and natural materials available in autumn bring rich, fiery colors and a variety of textures to floral arrangements. Seasonal foliage and berries, vines, dried flowers, seeds, nuts, gourds, and pumpkins all add dimension and interest. The palette of deep crimson, rust, gold, and orange introduces a warm ambience to your home as the temperature drops and outdoor colors fade.

WHITE
chrysanthemum
heather
rose

YELLOW / GOLD
bittersweet
chrysanthemum
celosia
gourds
rose
solidago
sunflower

PINK / RED
celosia
hypericum berries
pepper berries
rose

BURGUNDY
amaranthus
dahlia
hypericum berries

COPPER / RUST / ORANGE
amaranthus
bittersweet
Chinese lanterns
dahlia
miniature calla lily
pumpkin
safflower
sandersonia

LAVENDER / PURPLE
dahlia
heather

BLUE
hydrangea
thistle

GREEN
gourds
hypericum berries
seeded eucalyptus

October Dinner

This delightful centerpiece bursts with warm, rich colors. The hollowed-out pumpkin is an inexpensive but striking seasonal container. Cut crystal and pewter table accessories sparkle against the room's dark paneling. This party design can easily be expanded for a traditional Thanksgiving gathering.

flowers & natural materials

1 medium pumpkin

6 stems pepper berries

3 small apples

2 small pears

8 stems sandersonia

8 stems green amaranthus

15 stems assorted orange, rust, and
    golden yellow roses

6 stems deep red spray roses

10 stems copper calla lilies

5 or 6 stems of green foliage

supplies

floral foam

4" wired wood picks

6" unwired wood picks

 flower style

Napkin nosegays are easy to make and always add impressive detail to your tabletop. Use a few stems of berries and small flowers tied with raffia or ribbon to dress up a simple napkin.

1. While the floral foam is soaking, prepare the pumpkin. Cut off the top of the pumpkin and discard. Remove all the seeds from the interior; leaving a wide opening. Fill the pumpkin with soaked floral foam, extending it above the top (figure 1). If you are using a small pumpkin cut the foam to fit. If the pumpkin is very round push a few extra pieces of foam down to fill the space (figure 2).

figure 1

figure 2

2. Attach wired picks to stem end of pepper berries.

3. Pierce bottoms of the apples and pears with pointed ends of unwired wood picks.

4. Insert fruit into the foam at edge of the pumpkin and pepper berries to cascade down the side (figure 3).

figure 3

5. Add the sandersonia in the center of the foam; they will be the tallest flowers.

6. Fill out the arrangement with the amaranthus, roses, and spray roses.

7. The callas should be added to extend past the roses, giving movement to the design. You may find it helpful to reinforce the stems with 4" wired picks before inserting into the foam.

8. Finish with foliage as needed to fill.

Golden Glow Thanksgiving

Every element of this sumptuous Thanksgiving table is carefully planned to create a beautifully glowing, coordinated design. The softened colors and use of gold dress the table for an elegant meal. Meticulous attention shows in every detail, from the tiered centerpiece to the gilded pear place-card holders. The contrast of colors, textures, and shapes will delight your guests.

flowers & natural materials

23 pears (includes 8 for place card holders)

8 small pomegranates (dried pomegranates may be purchased at crafts stores)

8 artichokes (5 small, 3 large)

8 stems mauve roses

3 or 4 stems lemon leaves

assorted fresh herbs: sage, rosemary, oregano, thyme (if your herbs have flowering stems, use them also)

8 small bunches champagne grapes

10 kumquats

12 fresh or artificial berries (crafts stores have a great selection)

5 figs (artificial figs may be purchased at crafts stores)

small seasonal accents: safflower, red berries, pepper berries, thistles

supplies

antique-gold paint (spray can or small jar)

8 water tubes, 2" long

3-tiered serving dish

gold marking pen

1/4" waterproof floral tape

Centerpiece

1. To gild the pears, pomegranates, and artichokes, lightly spray with gold paint. The natural coloring of the fruit and artichokes should be visible through the gold. If using paint from a jar, rub it lightly over the surface with a rag to create highlights—don't brush it on to cover the fruit completely. Leave a few pears ungilded for contrast. Set aside 8 gilded pears for place-card holders.

2. Starting on bottom tier, arrange about half the lemon leaves and herbs around the edge (figure 1).

figure 1

3. Cut rose stems short and insert in water tubes.

4. Place 3 pears, 2 pomegranates, 3 artichokes, and 2 clusters of grapes around the bottom tier. Add 3 roses in water tubes (figure 2).

figure 2

5. Distribute the remaining roses, leaves, pears, pomegranates, and artichokes on the 2 top tiers as pictured.

6. Add clusters of grapes to fill in and drape over the edges of the 2 top tiers.

7. Working over all 3 tiers, distribute the kumquats, berries, figs, and seasonal accents. Insert sprigs of herbs for interest.

Place Card Holders

1. Write guests' names on lemon leaves using gold marking pen.

2. Cut a small slice from the rounded part of each of 8 gilded pears, so they sit flat on the plates. Scoop out a narrow hole in the opposite side of each; this will be the top (figure 1).

figure 1

3. Make 8 nosegays of herbs, small flowers, and berries; cut stems and secure with floral tape. Put a small amount of water in the hole in each pear and insert nosegays deep enough to hide taped stems.

4. Cut a small slit on the top of each pear, at the side of the nosegay, to insert personalized lemon leaves.

Asian Flair

This sophisticated centerpiece uses a traditional autumn palette in softened tones. The graceful flared vase is complemented by the lines of the flowers and foliage, with cascading bittersweet to provide a sense of movement.

flowers & natural materials

6–8 stems foliage with or without berries
(ruscus, pittosporum, rosehips, ming fern,
or cuttings from the garden)

12 stems orange lilies

6 stems ivory sarracenia lilies

2 or 3 stems bittersweet with berries

supplies

chicken wire

vase

figure 1

1. Cut a piece of chicken wire about 2" larger than the opening of your vase. Carefully fold edges under and position in vase just below the rim (figure 1). This will form a grid to hold the flowers in place. Fill the vase with water.

2. Create the basic shape of the arrangement with foliage. Position 6 stems of orange lilies to curve over the sides of the vase (figure 2). Add the sarracenia toward the center. Use the remaining orange lilies to add color in the center. Fill in with the remaining foliage and berries.

3. Place the completed arrangement on the table and add the bittersweet vines to trail, gracefully breaking the straight lines of the vase.

figure 2

Welcome Home

This impressive welcoming door swag made of vibrant fresh materials starts with a base of long-lasting evergreen, lemon leaves, and pinecones. The base of the easy-to-make coordinating topiary is a purchased ivy plant.

Door Swag

flowers & natural materials

pine branches

1 bunch lemon leaves

10 pinecones

14 small apples (fresh or artificial)

20 stems red-orange hypericum berries

5 stems Chinese lanterns

20 stems orange kangaroo paws

supplies

wire coat hanger and wire cutter

18-gauge spool wire

4" wired wood picks

6" unwired wood picks

hot-glue gun

bells (If you don't have an old-fashioned set of sleigh bells like those pictured, hang a few large bells from colorful ribbons.)

1. Cut coat hanger and bend it into a half circle. Tightly bind the pine branches to the wire base using spool wire, working from each end to the center. Add lemon leaves to fill out the shape and add width. (If you are making the swag to hang on a door, make sure the width is less than that of the door.) Make a wire loop at the center for hanging (figure 1).

figure 1

2. Using 6" unwired wood picks, hot-glue one to the stem end of each pinecone and insert one into each apple.

3. Add apples and pinecones. Fill out the shape of the swag with hypericum berries, securing each item with a dab of hot glue as you insert picks and stems. This will hold the materials firmly in place as the door is opened and closed.

4. Reinforce the stems of Chinese lanterns and kangaroo paws with wired picks. Push firmly into the base of pine, using a dot of hot glue to secure.

5. Attach the bells from a wire in the center of the swag. Hang the swag on the door.

6. Mist frequently to keep the fresh materials from drying out.

Topiary

flowers & natural materials

12 small pinecones

20 small apples (fresh or artificial)

25 stems red-orange hypericum berries

18 stems golden orange roses

8 stems orange kangaroo paws

1 bunch dried red globe amaranth

3 stems Chinese lanterns

supplies

one double-ball ivy topiary

terra-cotta or decorative pot if needed

20–30 water tubes, 2" long

4" wired and unwired wood picks

hot-glue gun

1. Hot-glue pinecones to unwired picks. Insert unwired picks into bottom of apples.

2. Cut hypericum, roses, and kangaroo paws into short lengths. Insert stems into water tubes making small clusters. Reinforce globe amaranth with wired picks (figure 1). Chinese lanterns and globe amaranth will dry naturally. Insert prepared materials directly into the ivy balls of the topiary. There will be a wire or twig frame under the ivy to provide support.

figure 1

3. Position a few pinecones, apples and hypericum berries at the base of the topiary, inserting the picks and stems through the ivy directly into the soil (figure 2).

4. Divide and distribute the remaining materials around the two balls of the topiary.

figure 2

Fireside Buffet

Simple branches contrast with bright berries and fresh fruit in this modest yet striking centerpiece. The design can easily be adapted for a larger space—branches are great fill material and can add dramatic height. Select the container to coordinate with the style of your room: a glass cylinder like the one shown here fits well with a contemporary décor; a large earthenware jug would be at home in a country-style room.

flowers & natural materials

3–4 birch branches

3 large pomegranates

branches with and without fruit, berries, or foliage (rose hips, apple, pear, blackberry, dogwood, bittersweet, hypericum)

supplies

heavy cylindrical vase approximately 8" wide x 8" tall

6" unwired wood picks

1. Bend or break birch branches to fit in glass vase. This will create support for tall or heavy branches (figure 1). Fill the vase with water.

figure 1

2. Insert one pick in the bottom of each pomegranate.

3. Position the tallest branches first, then fill out the shape with the remaining branches. Any branches that have heavy fruit should be near the rim of the vase.

4. Add the pomegranates and fill in with berries for color.

Dried-flower Crafts

When the days get short and the temperatures are too cool for fresh flowers from the garden, dried flowers are a lovely way to continue enjoying the beauty of nature's gifts. Dried-flower arrangements are not everlasting, but with proper care they should last up to six months. All dried flowers should be kept out of direct sunlight to prevent fading. Keep them dust free by gently cleaning with a soft paintbrush or small feather duster. When colors are no longer vibrant and petals begin to crumble, toss the flowers and create a new arrangement.

Rose and Bow Mini Flowerpots

flowers

1 small dried hydrangea head for each pot

1 or 2 dried roses or peonies for each pot

supplies

3" terra-cotta flowerpots

scraps of floral foam

6"–8" long pieces of wired ribbon

green chenille stems

4" wired wood picks

1. Fill the pots with floral foam to just below the rim. If you are using dry floral foam reinforce the brittle stems of the dried hydrangea and roses with wired picks. You can also use wet floral foam, unsoaked, for small projects like this. It is much softer and will not break fragile stems.

2. Fill the pots with hydrangea and then add the roses, inserting picks into foam (figure 1).

3. Tie the ribbon in a simple single knot and cut the ends in a fishtail design. Attach a chenille stem or wired pick and insert directly into the floral foam.

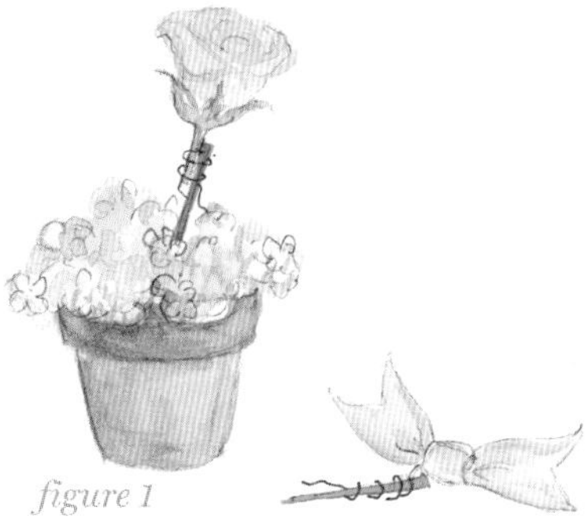

figure 1

Peony and Pepper Berry Basket

flowers & natural materials

3 dried peonies or roses

5 small dried hydrangea heads

3 clusters of pepper berries

15 stems dried lavender

dried lemon leaves

supplies

small decorative wire basket

green sheet moss to line basket

1/4 block dry floral foam (or a piece about 3" × 3" × 2")

4" wired wood picks

1. Line the basket to the rim with sheet moss. Place the floral foam in the lined basket to extend 1/2" above the rim.

2. Attach peonies, hydrangea, and pepper berries to wired picks.

3. Place hydrangea first, then peonies. Cluster lavender and insert stems into the floral foam. Tuck lemon leaves to fill.

4. Finish by adding a few clusters of pepper berries to cascade over the edge of the basket.

Autumn Wedding in the Woods

A rustic chapel in the woods sets the stage for an intimate outdoor ceremony. The simple white chair covers add a crisp note against the warm tones of the wooden building and autumn foliage. The covers pull off after the ceremony to reveal gilt ballroom chairs to use at the reception.

Bride's Bouquet

The bride carries an armful of vibrant roses, seasonal flowers, and berries. The stems are beautifully wrapped with ribbons and detailed with pearl pins to pick up the warm peach color of the berries.

flowers

7 stems copper amaranthus

6 stems coral roses

4 stems terra-cotta roses

10 stems peach hypericum berries

7 stems copper miniature calla lilies

7 stems seeded eucalyptus

5 stems orange dahlias

supplies

$1/2$" waterproof floral tape

rust ribbon $3/4$" wide

moss green ribbon $1/4$" wide

peach-colored pearl-headed pins

1. Remove all foliage from stems and separate flowers by type. Cut the seeded eucalyptus into small pieces and remove all leaves. Let flowers drink in a cool place several hours or overnight.

2. This hand-tied bouquet is not made in a round shape. Start the bouquet with 3 stems amaranthus, 2 roses, and 1 stem hypericum berry and secure with tape (figure 1).

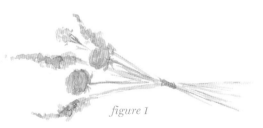

figure 1

3. Add more flowers in clusters, working back from the starting cluster, to create the slightly elongated shape of this presentation-style bouquet (figure 2).

figure 2

4. Secure stems as you work, until all flowers are used. Finish with a collar of seeded eucalyptus at the base of the bouquet. Tightly bind the stems with tape and cut to desired length.

5. Carefully lay the bouquet on its side (or have someone hold it for you) and wrap the stems with the rust colored ribbon. Secure at top and bottom with pins. Make a braid of moss green ribbon, securing with a pearl pin at each cross (photo, page 108).

Groom's Boutonniere

flowers

3 small pieces seeded eucalyptus

1 copper miniature calla lily

1 small cluster of peach hypericum berries

supplies

22-gauge straight wire

light green corsage tape

straight pins

boutonniere pins

6" piece of 1/4" wide rust ribbon

12" piece of 1/8" wide moss green satin ribbon

1. Wire all the flowers (page 32) and wrap stems with tape.

2. Position eucalyptus around the calla lily and twist stems together. Add the hypericum berries and wrap with tape to make one smooth stem.

3. Cut stems to 2" and wrap with rust ribbon. Secure ribbon at back with a straight pin.

4. To secure the green ribbon, insert a straight pin up through the stem end of the boutonniere. Twist the ribbon up and around the stem as pictured. Make a decorative loop and secure with straight pin at the top, just below the flowers. Add a lapel pin.

Table Candelabra

flowers

(quantities are for one candelabra)

15 stems "antique" hydrangea

10 stems burgundy hypericum berries

5 stems seeded eucalyptus

12 stems peach roses

10 stems crimson or rust-colored roses

8 pieces ivy

10 preserved orange or quince slices

supplies

green chenille stems

4 floral foam igloos 2$\frac{1}{2}$"–3" diameter

candelabra 28"–36" tall, one per table

22-gauge straight wire

5 pillar candles 3" × 6" or as needed for
candelabra

1. Using chenille stems, attach 3 soaked igloos to
   candelabra (figure 1).

figure 1

2. Using about 12 stems of hydrangea, work all around the candelabra, using all 3 igloos.

3. Add 9 stems of hypericum berries and most of the eucalyptus to fill.

4. Position 20 roses so colors are distributed all around. Insert ivy under the hydrangea to cascade down; twirl around the candelabra. Accent with wired orange slices.

5. Set the candelabra in place on table and add the candles. The candle cups often have small spikes to hold the candles firmly, or use candle adhesive or hot glue as needed to secure the candles.

6. In the remaining igloo make a low clustered arrangement with 1 or 2 stems of hydrangea, 1 stem of hypericum berries, 2 roses, and a few of eucalyptus. Place at the base of the candelabra (figure 2).

figure 2

✵ flower style

The centerpiece pictured uses 3" diameter pillar candles. Event sites often require that candle flames be enclosed. Simply change the candles to 2" diameter and enclose in glass sleeves or hurricanes.

Chair Garlands

These garlands add a lovely detail to the bride and groom's chairs.

flowers & natural materials

(quantities are for two chairs)

6 stems peach roses

10 preserved orange or quince slices
(available at craft shops)

10 stems lemon leaves

6 stems seeded eucalyptus

10 stems burgundy hypericum berries

8 small bunches red/orange seasonal leaves

supplies

18- and 22-gauge green spool wire

18-gauge straight wire

light green corsage tape

4 yards sheer wired gold ribbon
1"–1$^1/_2$" wide

1. Prepare roses with stem wire and corsage tape (page 32). Wire orange slices as illustrated (figure 1).

figure 1

2. Cut a 30" length of 18-gauge spool wire; make a loop at one end.

3. Cut lemon leaf stems into short pieces and make a garland by wiring clusters to the loop end. Work toward the opposite end, adding orange slices, eucalyptus, berries, and roses with 22-gauge spool wire (figure 2). Add leaves for contrast.

figure 2

4. When the garland is the desired length, make a loop at the opposite end to finish. Place loops of the completed garland on the finials of the chair. Tie 1 yard of ribbon around each finial and make a bow to hide the wire loops (figure 3). Make the second garland.

figure 3

winter

Winter is a season of celebrations, bringing opportunities to create festive floral designs to give as gifts and to use at home. Many favorite flowers are available year-round. When combined with seasonal greens like holly, pine, and berried blue spruce, the results are colorful displays that will bring pleasure throughout the holidays.

WHITE
amaryllis
bouvardia
heather
lily
paperwhite
narcissus
ranunculus
star of Bethlehem

YELLOW / GOLD
chrysanthemum
freesia
rose

PEACH / CORAL
carnation
chrysanthemum
rose

PINK / RED
amaryllis
bouvardia
berries
carnation
lily
rose

LAVENDER / PURPLE
dried lavender
freesia
statice

BLUE
berried blue spruce
statice

GREEN
cedar
dendrobium orchid
magnolia
ivy
moss
pine
seeded eucalyptus

Family Gathering

This handsome table setting features the traditional colors of the season with ever-greens and colorful sparkling ornaments. Use your favorite crystal compote or footed bowl as the focal point. The low pieces on each side of the compote feature stargazer lilies and red berries in a bed of greens. The expensive lilies are used sparingly and can easily be removed and replaced to keep the table decor fresh throughout the holiday season. To adapt this design to a longer table, add more low floral pieces and candlesticks. For a round dining table, surround the center display with 3 or 4 small floral pieces and votive candles. To complete the festive look, embellish each place setting with a nosegay of fresh pine and two ornaments: in this case, a piece of "crystallized" fruit and a whimsical bird, as take home gifts for your guests.

flowers & natural materials

several branches pine and cedar

4 stems stargazer lilies

6 stems red berries

10 stems statice

supplies

compote or footed bowl

"crystallized" fruit ornaments or ornaments of your choice (to fill bowl and one for each place setting)

2 6" floral dishes or saucers

1 block floral foam

$1/4$" waterproof floral tape

bird ornaments or ornaments of your choice (one for each place setting)

10 yards wired red satin ribbon 1" wide

$2^{1}/2$" wired wood picks

❀ flower style

It is not necessary to buy floral containers for centerpieces. Use your favorite pieces of crystal, silver, or china. Be creative: An ice bucket is perfect for a large display; set up a row of small pitchers on an oblong table; or cluster a few antique goblets around a simple glass vase.

1. Fill the compote or bowl with fruit ornaments. Accent with small sprigs of pine and cedar.

2. Prepare the floral dishes with soaked floral foam (figure 1).

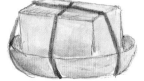

figure 1

3. Insert greens to create an oval shape on each floral dish (figure 2).

figure 2

4. Cut lily stems into 2 or 3 pieces each and insert through greens into the floral foam. Add berries and statice to fill.

5. Cut the ribbon to two 1-yard lengths and attach one end to a wired pick. Insert pick into the center bowl and bend the wired ribbon to form loops. Cascade the ribbon to the side arrangements. Accent the completed table with candlesticks or votives.

6. Cut remaining ribbon to 28" lengths. For each place setting, tie a sprig of cedar with ribbon and position ornaments as pictured on the plates.

Candlelight Dessert Buffet

Host a candlelight dessert buffet early in December to launch the holiday season in style. A good florist will have a selection of white flowers to add to your arrangement: pictured on page 120 are lisianthus, star of Bethlehem, paperwhites, and lilacs. You could also use roses, spray roses, ranunculus, and heather. Frame the display with dark glossy leaves, holiday greens, and bright berries.

flowers & natural materials

2 or 3 small flowering paperwhite plants
   in 3" pots

2 or 3 stems magnolia leaves (or enough
   to surround the base)

4 stems Casablanca lilies

6 stems star of Bethlehem

6 stems white lilac

10 stems red astilbe or sprays of berries

supplies

9" floral dish

1 block floral foam

$1/4$" waterproof floral tape

4 white taper candles 15" or 18" tall

 flower style

Star of Bethlehem is a very long-lasting flower. Each bud on the soft green spike opens to reveal a tiny white star-shaped flower.

1. Cut 2 pieces, each about 1¹/₂" wide, from the end of the block of soaked foam (figure 1). Make a setup as pictured, securing with floral tape.

figure 1

2. Cut 2 holes in the large piece of foam to hold the flower pots. Press the pots of paperwhites firmly into the foam (figure 2).

figure 2

3. Insert magnolia leaves all around the foam base to create a "wreath" that will frame the completed arrangement (figure 3).

4. Press candles into foam as positioned in photo.

5. Position lilies facing out from the flowerpots.

figure 3

6. Fill in with more leaves. Add star of Bethlehem in the center for height. Finish with lilacs and astilbe (or berries).

Pastel Christmas

This table is decorated with a sophisticated mix of flowers not usually associated with the holiday season: pink peonies, frosty white brunia, exotic pale green dendrobium orchids and spiky leucadendron flowers. The berried blue spruce and seeded eucalyptus add a traditional touch.

flowers &
natural materials

3 stems seeded eucalyptus

10 stems leucadendron

8 stems golden yellow roses

7 stems pink peonies

5 stems brunia

3 stems green dendrobium orchids

1 branch berried blue spruce

supplies

ornate glass compote or footed bowl

Spanish moss

1 block floral foam

1/4" waterproof floral tape

figure 1

1. Line the compote with Spanish moss and fill it with soaked floral foam; secure the foam to the bowl with tape (figure 1).

2. Cut the eucalyptus and insert into the foam to establish a "rounded" shape. Add leucadendron close to the foam.

3. Add roses and peonies in clusters of 2 or 3 flowers. This gives the arrangement a more natural look and emphasizes the colors. Add the silvery white balls of brunia as contrast against the greens.

4. Cut each orchid stem into 2 or 3 pieces and insert into the arrangement.

5. Position the completed arrangement on the table and form a wreath around the base of the compote with small pieces of berried blue spruce.

❋ flower style

If you have trouble finding peonies in the winter, buy the freeze-dried variety. Many seasonal flowers are now preserved for easy availability all year.

Festive Dinner Party

Dainty floral and herb nosegays serve as favors for a special holiday dinner. Hand-tied nosegays can be made in advance and travel well if you are making them away from the party site. The deep red tablecloth and soft green menu card are a contemporary take on the traditional holiday colors and pick up floral shades in the bouquets.

flowers &
natural materials

(for one nosegay)

8 stems roses in assorted warm colors

8 stems miniature carnations

5 stems deep purple statice

1 stem dill cut in short pieces

6 stems assorted herbs (sage, rosemary, thyme, oregano are good choices)

supplies

1/2" waterproof floral tape

6" paper or lace doily (one for each nosegay)

3" glass bubble bowl or other small vase (one for each plate)

1. Remove all foliage from roses. Separate flowers by type and place in buckets of water. Allow time for roses and carnations to open in floral preservative. The charm of this nosegay is that the flowers are fully open, displayed at their peak perfection.

2. Make a hand-tied nosegay, starting with a stem each of rose, carnation, and statice (figure 1). Turn the nosegay as you work, adding the remaining flowers and herbs to create a round shape. Add the dill for textural contrast.

figure 1

3. Tape stems securely to hold bouquet.

4. Cut an X in the doily and insert the stems (figure 2). Push the doily up to frame the nosegay. Cut stems before placing it in a vase filled with water.

figure 2

Everlasting Roses

Attractive and long-lasting, these dried-flower projects are very easy to make and require only a few materials. The wreath uses tiny rosebuds sold by the bag. The matching topiary uses a premade topiary form. Vary the colors and you can tailor the projects for any season. They make lovely gifts, especially when sprinkled with a few drops of rose oil for added impact.

Wreath

flowers

1 lb. bag dried red rosebuds

supplies

6" green dry foam wreath

2 yards red ribbon 3/4" wide

straight pins

hot-glue gun

1. Cut a 12" length of ribbon and pin a loop to what will be the top of the wreath. Secure with hot glue and another straight pin through the glue.

2. Working in small sections, carefully glue rosebuds to the form in concentric circles until the entire wreath is covered (figure 1).

3. Make a bow from the remaining ribbon (page 33) and pin it to the top of the wreath.

figure 1

☀ flower style

If the wreath will be hung in a window or on a glass door, completely cover the foam wreath form. If the wreath will only be seen from one side, work about three quarters of the way around, leaving the back flat for hanging against a wall.

Rose Topiary

flowers

60–70 dried or preserved red rose heads

supplies

12" tall green dry foam topiary form

pot for topiary if needed (terra-cotta, ceramic, or decorative urn)

hot-glue gun

green sheet moss

1. Glue the foam base of the topiary (figure 1) into the pot you have chosen. You may want to add a few rocks for weight so the topiary is not top-heavy when completed.

2. Working one section at a time, hot-glue the rose heads to the topiary form.

3. To complete, glue the moss in place to hide the foam base (figure 2).

figure 1

figure 2

 flower style

For a more rustic variation, glue green moss to the surface of the wreath or topiary form before adding the roses. The moss will show through between the roses, adding color and texture contrast.

To My Valentine

A stunning heart of fresh velvety roses takes it shape from a decorative wire basket. The deep red roses are intensified by the contrast of a few pastel blooms and the delicate greenery frames the basket with a playful touch.

flowers

50–60 stems red roses

10 stems assorted pale pink or cream
    sweetheart or spray roses

6 pieces small-leaved ivy or smylax

supplies

heart-shaped wire basket about 10" wide

plastic wrap or cellophane to line basket

green sheet moss

2 blocks floral foam

1. Strip the foliage from the rose stems and place in water. Let the roses drink until the heads start to open.

2. Press small pieces of moss all around the sides of the wire basket.

3. Line the basket with plastic wrap or heavy cellophane.

4. Completely fill the basket with soaked floral foam, cutting the pieces to fit snugly. The floral foam should sit just below the rim of the basket (figure 1).

figure 1

5. Cut the stems of all the roses so the heads will sit just above the rim of the basket. Starting in the center, insert the red roses very close together to completely cover the floral foam. Accent the edges with small pink roses.

6. Tuck pieces of ivy all around the edge of the basket to soften the shape.

❋ flowerstyle

When buying roses for the Valentine heart, be sure to ask for short-stemmed varieties. They will be less expensive than long-stemmed roses. An arrangement made of very short-stemmed flowers, like this rose heart, will benefit from frequent misting.

Brighten the Day

This big, beautiful floral display will brighten your home and lift your spirits during the dreariest winter months. The colorful fruit and roses glow with warmth, while the clouds of hydrangea add a soft fullness. Remember to change the water frequently to prevent decay. A few drops of bleach in the water will keep it sparkling.

flowers & natural materials

red apples or pears to fill vase

30 stems roses in assorted colors and sizes (red, orange, pink, cream, and two-tone varieties)

20 stems burgundy and/or "antique" hydrangea

6–8 stems small, graceful green foliage (pittosporum, ivy, or cut snips from a houseplant)

supplies

glass vase approximately 10" tall

figure 1

1. Fill the vase half full of water and add fruit.

2. Begin by placing the taller roses and hydrangea in the center; the fruit will act as a grid to hold the stems in place (figure 1).

3. Work around the vase adding more roses and hydrangea, cutting stems to vary the height of the flowers. Finish by adding foliage for contrast and fill vase with water.

Pomanders

Aromatic pomanders can be hung on a Christmas tree or placed throughout the house for color and fragrance. Many pomanders are made from items found in the kitchen: citrus fruits, cloves, and cinnamon sticks are good things to start with. Other materials that work well are dried lavender, preserved quince or orange slices, tiny pinecones, seeds, and mosses, with accents of ribbon and raffia.

Fruit and Herb Bundles

1. Stack 3 or 4 slices of preserved orange or quince and tie together with raffia.

2. Slide a small piece of lavender or rosemary under the knot or tie a small cinnamon stick in the raffia.

3. A small bunch of dried lavender or a few cinnamon sticks tied with raffia or ribbon adds a nice contrast to your display.

Citrus Pomanders

1. To create decorative patterns in fresh oranges, lemons, or limes use a sharp paring knife to cut thin strips from the surface of the peel. Insert cloves into the exposed white skin of the fruit following the patterns.

figure 1

2. Display pomanders in a decorative bowl.

Winter Wonderland Wedding

This Christmas wedding combines holiday themes with wedding traditions to create a grand floral display in a formal room decorated in an opulent yet inviting style. On the console table, crystal candelabra sparkle next to miniature Christmas trees. A large gilt mirror is swagged with holiday greens and crimson ribbons as a paper maché angel watches over all.

Bride's Bouquet

The velvety red roses highlight the delicacy of the cream sweetheart roses.

flowers

18 stems large red roses

10 stems red sweetheart roses

10 stems cream sweetheart roses

8 stems white stock

2 or 3 pieces of variegated ivy

supplies

1/2" waterproof floral tape

2 yards white satin ribbon 1" wide

7 pearl-headed pins

1. Strip the foliage from flowers and place in water. Let the flowers drink in a cool place several hours or overnight until they begin to open. The bouquet will be more interesting if flowers are at different stages of development.

2. Start the bouquet with 3 stems red roses and 1 stem red sweetheart rose. As you work, turn the bouquet, adding a few clusters of cream roses and stock to break up the solid red. Use all the flowers to create a round, full hand-tied bouquet (page 30).

3. When you are happy with the shape, add a few sprigs of ivy and tightly bind the stems with tape and clip to the desired length.

4. Starting at the bottom, firmly wrap stems with satin ribbon. At the top, cut the ribbon and neatly fold under, securing with a pearl pin. Use additional pearl pins to stud the length of the ribbon wrapped bouquet stem.

Groom's Boutonniere

flowers

1 stem red rose

1 stem red sweetheart rose

1 stem white stock, buds only

a few perfect ivy leaves

supplies

18-gauge straight wire

28-gauge spool wire

light green corsage tape

boutonniere pin

1. Wire the rose with straight wire and the stock and ivy with spool wire (page 32).

2. Using the large red rose as the foundation flower, position the smaller flowers and twist stems together.

3. Wrap with tape to create a single smooth stem 3"–4" long and twist around pencil to form a tendril. Add pin to secure to lapel.

Table Decor

Table flowers are kept low and full for intimacy. Framed family photographs and silver candlesticks add nostalgic notes.

flowers & natural materials

(for one 60' round table)

34 stems red roses

20 stems white roses

10 stems red spray roses

12 stems white bouvardia

assorted seasonal foliage (pine, cedar, lemon leaves)

supplies

9" floral dish

1 block floral foam

$^1/_4$" waterproof floral tape

4 yards sheer silver wired ribbon 1" wide

4" wired wood picks

4 small glass or silver vases

4 silver candlesticks

4 white taper candles 12" or 15"

2 silver picture frames

10–12 tiny silver heart-shaped ornaments

1. Prepare floral dish with soaked foam (figure 1) and create a base of greens to cover the setup.

figure 1

2. Using 30 stems red roses, 12 stems white roses, and 6 stems red spray roses, add to the arrangement in single color clusters of 3 to 5 stems. This should cover most of the floral foam (figure 2).

3. Fill in with 4 stems bouvardia and bits of foliage cut short.

figure 2

4. Cut the ribbon into 18" lengths and make 8 bows. Attach a 4" wired pick to each bow (page 141) and secure in the arrangement. The silver heart ornaments are also secured with wired picks.

5. Make nosegays for the small vases using 1 stem red rose, 2 stems white rose, 1 stem red spray rose, 2 stems bouvardia, and a few small bits of greenery for each. Tape the nosegays, clip stems and place in small vases filled with water.

6. Arrange the floral and decorative elements on the tabletop as diagrammed (figure 3).

figure 3

Index